Purim Is a Time for Fun

פּורים איז אַ
שפּיל אַזאַ

Book by Miriam Hoffman
Art by Tsirl (Cecelia) Waletzky
Music by Malke Gottlieb

Coral Springs, Florida
www.YILoveJewish.org

Copyright © 2021 Oyfgang

Originally published by OYFGANG, New York, 1968

All rights reserved. No portion of this book may be reproduced mechanically, electronically, or by any other means, including photocopying, without written permission of the publisher. It is illegal to copy this book, post it to a website, or distribute it by any other means without permission from the publisher.

Print ISBN: 978-0-9993365-7-1

Layout by Gary A. Rosenberg • www.garyarosenberg.com

Printed in the United States of America

Song #1
PURIM PLAYERS

Purim players on their way,
From far away they're drumming!
From street to street throughout the land,
From ancient times forthcoming.

In Shushan Town a masquerade,
You hear the Graggers thunder.
A parade, a carnaval,
Shalakh Mones sweets asunder!

A trick, a joke, a game so fun;
From way, way back and under,
So open up and let us in—
These actors are a wonder!

Spoken:
The King is sleeping on the throne.
Wake him up. Let it be known:
"Akhashveyrush, here's the news:
Quickly, quick—put on your shoes!
Grab your pants and grab your crown,
Purim Players are in town!"

The King, he scratches his fair head—
"When I'm asleep, who guards my bed?"

Did you call, my royal Highness?
Here I am, your Haman waits!
But your Queen, your Vashti's gone.
As the Megillah correctly states.

The King is losing his composure;
His crown is trembling on his head.
The entire palace trembles with him;
His voice fills the land with dread

"Catch her! Find her! I'm so perturbed.
My Purim will not be disturbed!"

Now, let it be known throughout the land,
His Majesty has one desire:
A brand new Queen, he now demands—
A beauty who will quell his fire.

Shushan City starts to shake,
Shushan City's full of fear.
Get him all the city's beauties,
Let them line up far and near.

Mordekhay the righteous does not wait,
As soon as he hears the news in state,
He says, "Esther, quickly! Dear, get ready!
The Megillah says we should be steady."

And to Akhashveyrush, the King!

Song #2
A GOOD PURIM

A good Purim, Purim, Purim!
A good Purim, a good year.

See, I'm bringing you your love bride,
See, I bring you love galore.

And the King says, sweet as honey,
"No prettier bride could I ever find—
She will be my newest Queen,
In love and joy we'll be aligned."

In the corner stands the scoundrel,
Full of envy, slick and sly.
On the King's side lovely Esther,
On the left stands Mordekhay.

Haman pulls his tiny whiskers
And his eyes are full of fear.
And he bows, he kneels, he's begging—
Whispering into the King's ear

Song #3
GREAT KING

"Majesty, your greatest Highness,
Let ears and nose hear what I say:
Jews are reading the Megillah,
They even read it the wrong way.

"Look at Mordekhay, twisting, turning,
He thinks he knows all, as he's plotting.

"He's preparing
'Hocus-Pocus'
Quietly, he says the word.
On you, he'll work his
evil magic—
He'll turn you into a
Koo-Koo bird!

And as soon as he
declares the word,
The King becomes a
Koo-Koo bird.

The Koo-Koo bird will squint its eyes,
Then, far, far, far away it flies.

When Koo-Koo birds want to sing,
They jump around and start to swing.
And so they lock him in his nest,
And then they tell him, "Sit and rest."

All are laughing ha, ha, ha!
Look at him, a fool; say Ahh...

The King then knows that times are bitter—
His trembling crown is all aquiver!

"Hang those Jews from towers high—
I'll spoil their Purim till they cry!"
As soon as he proclaims this news,
Esther stands and takes her cues:

Song #4
HAMAN, OPEN THE DOOR

Haman! Open wide the door,
You try to hurt me to the core.
Hear my heart, which you've defiled:
I, too, am a Jewish child.

You may hurt Jews far and wide;
But I, with them, the royal bride.
Haman! Open wide the door,
You try to hurt us to the core.

Spoken:
The King he shouts upon his throne,
"No! My Queen! LEAVE HER ALONE!
Now, bring in a Purim clown,
My proclamation is NEW in town—

"I proclaim TODAY IS PURIM:
Celebrate, make noise, be posh!

This is the end of evil Haman,
We'll make from him
a *Homentash!*

As declared, so will it be:
A poppy homentash we'll see;
Carried on a giant tray,
For the King, we'll all shout *Hooray!!!*

The King, he then did slice the cookie;
On top, below—it's time to eat.
Everyone did get a taste,
And said, "How good—how good
and sweet!"

Song #5—
Bells are Ringing

Bells are ringing, drums are drumming,
Cymbals cymbling, jesters, clowns!
Everyone is dancing round—
Purim, Purim—what a sound!

Honey flows right off the table,
Wine and food will hit the spot.
Jews have only a single Purim,
But evil Ha-amans? There's a lot . . .

Open all your windows wide,
Use your Graggers with great pride.
Dance around and Tra-La-Lun,
Purim Is a Time for FUN!

1. Purim Shpilers
(Purim Players)

2. A Gut Purim
(A Good Purim)

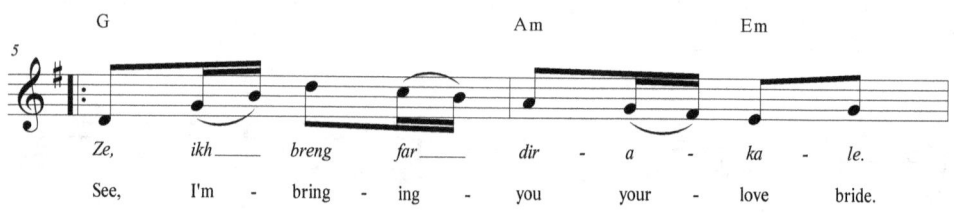
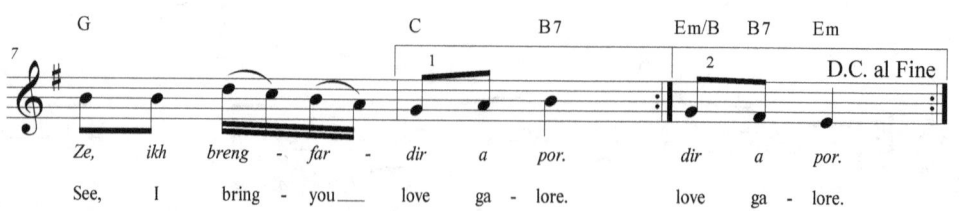

3. Groyser Meylekh
(Great King)

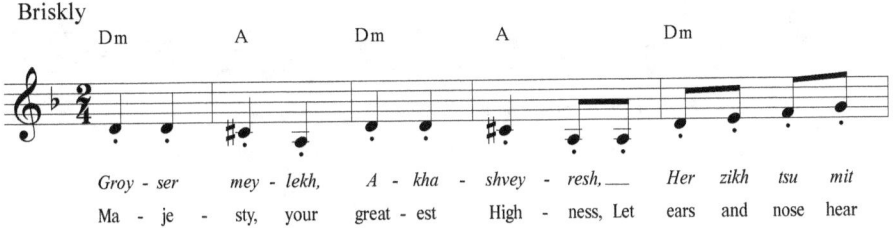

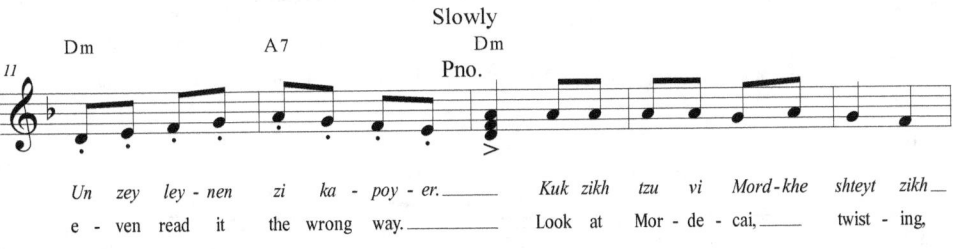

4. Homen, Efn Di Tir
(Haman, Open the Door)

5. Klingen Gleklekh
(Bells Are Ringing)

וואָקאַבולאַר
Vokabular
Vocabulary

Ahashverus	Akhashveyresh	אחשורוש
Vashti	Vashti	ושתּי
Esther	Ester	אסתּר
Mordecai the Just	Mordkhe Hatsadik	מרדכי הצדיק
Haman	Homen	המן
Shushan	Shushan	שושן
King	Meylekh	מלך
Queen	Malke	מלכּה
Book of Esther	Megile	מגילה
Gifts of cakes — sweets	Shalakh-Mones	שלח־מנות
3-Cornered Tart	Homen-Tash	המן־טאַש
Purim noise-maker	Grager	גראַגער
Jewish Holiday	Yontev	יום־טוב
Anger	Kas	כּעס
Bride	Kale	כּלה
Moustache	Vontses	וואָנצעס
Upside-Down	Kapoyer	קאַפּויער
Jesters	Lets-Leytsim	לץ — לצים
Noise	Rash	רעש
Clowns	Payatsn	פּאַיאַצן
End	Sof	סוף
With Good Luck	In a mazldiker sho	אין אַ מזלדיקער שעה

טיר און טויער עפֿנט ברייט,
מיט די גראַגערס אָנגעגרייט.
רונד אַרום און טראַ-לאַ-לאַ,
פּורים איז אַ שפּיל אַזאַ!

Tir un toyer efnt brayt
Mit di gragers ongegrayt
Rund arum un tra-la-la
Purim iz a shpiel aza

קלינגען גלעקלעך, פּויקן טאַצן!
צימבלען לצים און פּאַיאַצן!
טאַנצן אַלע אין אַ ראָד —
אין אַ פּורים־קאַראָהאָד.

Klingen gleklekh, poikn tatzn!
Tzimblen, leytzim un payatzn!
Tantzn aleh in a rod—
In a Purim karahod

גיסט זיך האָניק פֿון די טישן.
גיסט זיך ווײַן, עס פֿעלט קיין זאַך.
פּורים איז בײַ ייִדן איינער —
אָבער המנס גאָר אַ סך!

Gist zikh honik fun di tishn
Gist zikh vayn, es felt kayn zakh
Purim iz bay Yidn eyner—
Ober Homens—Gor a sakh!

Ot gezogt un shoyn geton—
A homentash mit zeesn mon—
Tzugetrogn oyf a tatz
Farn meylakh in palatz

אָט געזאָגט און שוין געטאָן—
אַ המן־טאַש מיט זיסן מאָן—
צוגעטראָגן אויף אַ טאַץ
פֿאַרן מלך אין פּאַלאַץ.

האָט דער מלך דאָס צעשניטן
אויבן, אונטן און אין מיטן;
יעדער האָט פֿאַרזוכט אַ ביס
און געזאָגט: "ווי גוט און זיס!"

Hot der meylakh dos tzeshnitn
Oybn, untn un in mitn;
Yeder hot farzukht a bis
Un gezogt: "Vi gut un zees!"

איך באַפֿעל הײַנט — יום־טוב פּורים —
גראַגערט, ייִדן! מאַכט אַ רעש —
און אַ סוף, דו בייזער המן!

Ikh bafel haynt—Yom Tov Purim—
Gragert Yidn! Makht a raash—
Un a sof, du beyzer Homen!

מאַכט פֿון אים —
אַ
המן־טאַש!"

Makht fun im—
a
Homentash"

שרײַט דער מלך אױפֿן טראָן:
„נײן! מײַן מלכּה רירט ניט אָן!
ברענגט אַרײַן אַ פּורים-לץ.
איך גיב אַרױס אַ נײַ געזעץ—

Shrayt der meylakh oyfn tron:
"Neyn! Mayn malkeh rirt nit on!
Brengt arayn a Purim leytz
Ikh gib aroys a nay gezetz—

„המן! עפֿן ברייט די טיר
און זוך אויס אַ בוים פֿאַר מיר —
הערט! איך זאָג אײַך אָן אַצינד
איך בין אויך אַ ייִדיש קינד.

Homen! Efn breyt di tir
Un zukh oys a boym far mir—
Hert! Ikh zog aykh on atzind
Ikh bin oykh a Yiddish kind

הענגען וועלן ייִדן אַלע,
און מיט זיי דעם קעניגס כּלה!"
„המן! עפֿן ברייט די טיר
און זוך אויס אַ בוים פֿאַר מיר —

Hengen veln Yidn aleh
Un mit zey dem keynigs kaleh
Homen! Efn breyt di tir
Un zukh oys a boym far mir—

זעט דער מלך אַז ס'איז ביטער,
גיט אויף אים די קרוין אַ ציטער:

Zeyt der meylakh az s'iz biter
Git oyf im di kroyn a tziter

„הענגט די ייִדן אויפֿן טורעם,
כ'וועל פֿאַרשטערן זייער פורים!"

"Hengt di Yidn oyfn turem,
Kh'vel farshteyrn zayer Purim!"

ווי ער גיט אזאַ באַפֿעל —
שטייט שוין אסתר אויפֿן שוועל:

Vi er git aza bafel—
Shteyt shoyn Esther oyfn shvel:

פֿינטלט קוקו מיט די אויגן —
זײַנען פֿײגל אָנגעפֿלויגן.

Pintlt Kuku mit di oygn—
Zaynen feygl ongefloygn

וויל דער קוקו עפּעס זינגען,
נעמען קוקו־פֿײגל שפּרינגען.
זעצט מען אים אַרײַן אין שטײַג
און מע זאָגט אים: "זיץ און שווײַג!"

Vil der Kuku epes zingen
Nemen Kuku foygl shpringen
Zetzt men im arayn in shtayg
Un m'zogt im: "Zitz un shvayg"

לאַכן אַלע: "כאַ־כאַ־כאַ.
קוקט אים אָן!
אַ נאַר אַזאַ".

Lakhn aleh: "Kha - Kha
- Kha
Kukt im on,
a nar aza"

ווי ער זאָגט אַרויס דאָס װאָרט,
װערט אַ קוקו אויפֿן אָרט!

Vi er zogt aroys dos vort,
Vert a Kuku oyfn ort

„גרויסער מלך אחשורוש,
הער זיך צו מיט נאז און אויער
יידן לייענען די מגילה
און זיי לייענען זי קאפויער.

Groyser meylakh Akhashveyrush
Her zikh tzu mit noz un oyer
Yidn leynen di Megillah
Un zey leynen zi kapoyer

קוק זיך צו ווי מרדכי שטייט זיך
און ער וויסט אלץ און ער גרייט זיך.

Kuk zikh tzu vi Mordkhe shteyt zikh
Un er veyst altz un er greyt zikh

ער וועט מאכן האקום־פאקום
שטילערהייט און פון דער ווייטן,
און דעם גרויסן אחשורוש —
אויף א קוקו־פויגל בייטן!"

Er vet makhn Hokus-Pokus
Shtilerhayt un fun der vaytn
Un dem groysn Akhashveyrush—
Oyf a Kuku-Foygl baytn!

שטייט אין ווינקל דער מיניסטער,
זעט דער מלך שײַנט פֿון פֿרייד.
פֿון דער רעכטער זײַט — די מלכּה,
פֿון דער לינקער — מרדכי שטייט.

Shteyt in vinkl der minister
Zeyt der meylakh shaynt fun freyd
Fun der rekhter zayt—Di malkeh
Fun der linker—Mordkheh shteyt

און ער דרייט די דינע וואָנצעס
און דאָס קרומע אייגל צאַפּלט.
און ער נייגט זיך, און ער בייגט זיך
און ער שושקעט און ער פּלאַפּלט:

Un er dreyt di dineh vontzes
Un dos krumeh eygl tzaplt
Un er neygt zikh, un er beygt zikh
Un er shushket un er plaplt

און צום מלך אחשוורוש:
Un tzum Meylakh Akhashveyrush:
„אַ גוט־פּורים, אַ גוט־יאָר!
A gut Purim, Purim, Purim
A gut Purim—A gut yor!
זע, איך ברענג פֿאַר דיר אַ כּלה —
זע, איך ברענג פֿאַר דיר אַ פּאָר".
Zeh, ikh breng far dir a kaleh
Zeh, ikh breng far dir a por

און דער מלך, זיס ווי האָניק,
זאָגט:,,קיין שענערס איז נישטאָ —
זי וועט זײַן די נײַע מלכּה —
אין אַ מזלדיקער שעה!"
Un der meylakh zees vi honik
Zogt: "Kayn sheners iz nishto—
Zi vet zayn di nayeh malkeh—
In a mazldikeh sho

מרדכי הצדיק ווארט ניט לאַנג.
ווי ער הערט דעם נייעם קלאַנג,
זאָגט ער: "אסתר! מאַך זיך גרייט,
ווי אין דער מגילה שטייט

Mordkheh Ha'Tzadik vart nit lang
Vi er hert dem nayem klang
Zogt er: "Esther, makh zikh greyt,
Vi in der megilleh shteyt

אוּן זאָל באַלד אַרויס אַ קלאַנג:
ס'האָט דער מלך אַ פֿאַרלאַנג.
ער זוכט אַ מלכּה שיין און פֿריילעך,
ווי עס פּאַסט זיך פֿאַר אַ מלך!

Un zol bald aroys a klang
S'hot der meylakh a farlang.
Er zukht a malkeh sheyn un fraylakh
Vi es past zikh far a meylakh

ווערט אין שושן אַ גערודער,
ווערט אין שושן אַ געלויף,
און די סאַמע שענסטע מיידלעך
אַלע קלײַבן זיך צונויף.

Vert in Shushan a geruder
Vert in Shushan a geloyf
Un di sameh shensteh meydlekh
Ale klaybn zikh tzunoif

ציטערט אַזש פֿון כּעס דער מלך,
צִיטערט אַזש די קרוין אויף אים.
צִיטערט אַזש דער גאַנצער פּאַלאַץ
פֿון זײַן ציטערדיקער שטים.

Tzitert aszh fun kaas der meylakh,
Tzitert aszh di kroyn oyf im
Tzitert aszh der gantzer palatz
Fun zayn tziterdiker shtim

„כאַפּט זי! הענגט זי אויפֿן טורעם!
שטערן וועט זי ניט מײַן פּורים!"

Khapt zi! Hengt zi oyfn turem!
Shteyrn vet zi nit mayn Purim!

קראַצט דער מלך זיך אין קאָפּ.
„אַז איך שלאָף — ווער היט מיך אָפּ?"

Kratzt der meylakh zikh in kop
"Az ikh shlof—Ver hit mikh op?"

„האָסט גערופֿן גרױסער מלך —
אָט בין איך דײַן המן גרײט!
נאָר דײַן ושתּי איז אַנטלאָפֿן —
ווי אין דער מגילה שטײט!

"Host gerufen groyser meylakh?—
Ot bin ikh dayn Homen grayt!
Nor dayn Vashti iz antlofn—
Vi in der megillah shteyt

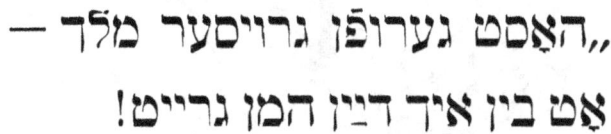

שלאָפֿט דער מלך אױפֿן טראָן —
װעקט אים אױף און זאָגט אים אָן:
„אחשורוש! גיכער, גיך —
צי אַרױף אױף זיך די שיך —
כאַפּ די הױזן,
כאַפּ די קרױן,
פּורים־שפּילערס קומען אָן."

Shloft der meylakh oyfn tron
Vekt im oyf un zogt im on:
"Akhashveyrush! Gikher gikh—
Tzi aroyf oyf zikh di shikh—
Khap di hoyzn, khap di kroyn
Purim Shpilers kumen on

אין שושן הײנט אַ מאַסקאַראַד.
מ'הערט דעם גראַגער רוישן.
אַ פּאַראַד, אַ קאַרנאַוואַל,
שלח-מנות פֿולע קוישן.

In Shushan haynt a masquerade
M'hert dem grager royshn
A parad, a karnaval
Shalekh mones fule koyshn

אַ קונץ, אַ וויץ, אַ שפּיל, אַ שפּאַס,
פֿון אַזוי פֿיל יאָרן —
מאַכט אויף! מאַכט אויף!
און לאָזט אַרײַן
די פֿרײלעכע אַקטיאָרן.

A kuntz, a vitz, a shpil, a shpas
Fun azoy fil yorn
Makht oyf! Makht oyf!
   Un lozt arayn
Di freylekhe aktyorn

פורים איז אַ שפּיל אַזאַ

Purim Iz a Shpiel Aza

פּורים־שפּילערס קומען אָן,
קומען פֿון דער װײַטן.
אַ גאַס אַרײַן, אַ גאַס אַרױס
פֿון אַלטע, אַלטע צײַטן.

Purim shpilers kumen on
Kumen fun der vaytn
A gas arayn, a gas aroys
Fun alte, alte tzaytn

A Division of Yiddishkayt Initiative

Coral Springs, Florida
www.YILoveJewish.org

Copyright © 2021 Oyfgang

Originally published by OYFGANG in NY, 1968

All rights reserved. No portion of this book may be reproduced mechanically, electronically, or by any other means, including photocopying, without written permission of the publisher. It is illegal to copy this book, post it to a website, or distribute it by any other means without permission from the publisher.

Print ISBN: 978-0-9993365-9-5

Layout by Gary A. Rosenberg • www.garyarosenberg.com

Printed in the United States of America

www.ingramcontent.com/pod-product-compliance
Lightning Source LLC
Chambersburg PA
CBHW050449010526
44118CB00013B/1745